NORTH AMERICAN ANIMALS

Mountain Goats

by Megan Borgert-Spaniol

BELLWETHER MEDIA · MINNEAPOLIS, MN

Note to Librarians, Teachers, and Parents:

Blastoff! Readers are carefully developed by literacy experts and combine standards-based content with developmentally appropriate text.

Level 1 provides the most support through repetition of high-frequency words, light text, predictable sentence patterns, and strong visual support.

Level 2 offers early readers a bit more challenge through varied simple sentences, increased text load, and less repetition of high-frequency words.

Level 3 advances early-fluent readers toward fluency through increased text and concept load, less reliance on visuals, longer sentences, and more literary language.

Level 4 builds reading stamina by providing more text per page, increased use of punctuation, greater variation in sentence patterns, and increasingly challenging vocabulary.

Level 5 encourages children to move from "learning to read" to "reading to learn" by providing even more text, varied writing styles, and less familiar topics.

Whichever book is right for your reader, Blastoff! Readers are the perfect books to build confidence and encourage a love of reading that will last a lifetime!

This edition first published in 2018 by Bellwether Media, Inc.

No part of this publication may be reproduced in whole or in part without written permission of the publisher. For information regarding permission, write to Bellwether Media, Inc., Attention: Permissions Department, 5357 Penn Avenue South, Minneapolis, MN 55419.

Library of Congress Cataloging-in-Publication Data

Names: Borgert-Spaniol, Megan, 1989- author.
Title: Mountain Goats / by Megan Borgert-Spaniol.
Description: Minneapolis, MN : Bellwether Media, Inc., [2018] | Series:
  Blastoff! Readers: North American Animals | Audience: Age 5-8. | Audience:
  K to grade 3. | Includes bibliographical references and index.
Identifiers: LCCN 2016052746 (print) | LCCN 2017009468 (ebook) | ISBN
  9781626176386 (hardcover : alk. paper) | ISBN 9781681033686 (ebook)
Subjects: LCSH: Mountain goat–Juvenile literature.
Classification: LCC QL737.U53 B684 2018 (print) | LCC QL737.U53 (ebook) | DDC
  599.64/75–dc23
LC record available at https://lccn.loc.gov/2016052746

Editor: Nathan Sommer   Designer: Josh Brink
Printed in the United States of America, North Mankato, MN.

Table of Contents

What Are Mountain Goats?

Mountain goats are hooved **mammals** that live in western North America. They are not true goats, but they are related.

In the Wild

N
W E
S

Extinct

Extinct in the Wild

Critically Endangered

Endangered

Vulnerable

Near Threatened

Least Concern

mountain goat range = ☐

conservation status: least concern

Mountain goats can be found from the western United States to northern Canada.

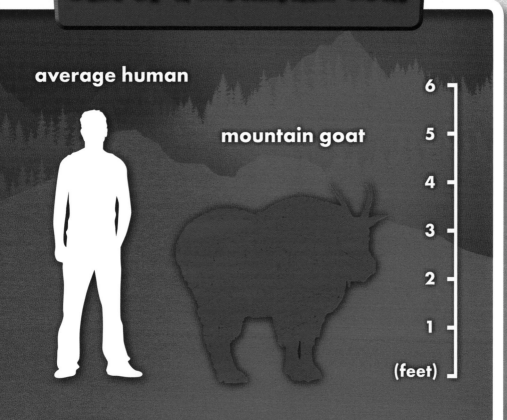

Size of a Mountain Goat

average human

mountain goat

6
5
4
3
2
1
(feet)

These mammals measure 3.5 feet (1 meter) tall at the shoulder. They can weigh up to 300 pounds (136 kilograms).

Males are usually larger
than females.

Climbing High

Mountain goats live high on mountains where most other animals cannot survive. They may live more than 10,000 feet (3,048 meters) above **sea level**.

They are the largest animals
to live at this **altitude**.

split hooves

Strong legs help mountain goats climb and jump from rock to rock. Some can travel nearly 12 feet (3.7 meters) in one leap!

Split hooves allow mountain goats to balance on steep rocks.

Surviving the Cold

Mountain goats grow thick double coats for the winter months. **Guard hairs** protect them from the wind and snow.

Identify a Mountain Goat

white coat   pointed horns   beard

They **shed** these woolly coats each spring and summer.

mountain heather

lingonberries

snowberries

black crowberries

Douglas fir

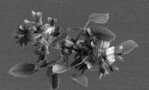

alfalfa

Mountain goats **graze** on what they can find high up in the mountains.

The **herbivores** mostly feed on grasses, mosses, and twigs. They also lick salt off of rocks on cliffs.

horns

Female mountain goats are called nannies. Males are called billies. Both have curved, pointed horns.

Males often use their horns to battle each other for females.

Nannies give birth to **kids** in spring. The babies can climb rocks a few days after birth. They stay close to mom to avoid golden eagles and other **predators**.

Baby Facts

Name for babies:	kids
Size of litter:	1 to 2 kids
Length of pregnancy:	5 to 6 months
Time spent with mom:	about 1 year

Kids live with their mom for about a year. She teaches them how to find food and stay safe on steep cliffs.

The kids also play together.
They love to jump on
one another!

Glossary

altitude—height above sea level

graze—to eat grasses and other plants on the ground

guard hairs—long, thick hairs on the outside of a mountain goat's coat

herbivores—animals that only eat plants

kids—baby mountain goats

mammals—warm-blooded animals that have backbones and feed their young milk

predators—animals that hunt other animals for food

sea level—the height of the surface of the sea

shed—to lose something on the body at the same time every year; mountain goats shed their coats.

split hooves—hooves that are split into two toes; hooves are hard coverings that protect the feet of some animals.

To Learn More

AT THE LIBRARY
Magby, Meryl. *Mountain Goats*. New York, N.Y.:
PowerKids Press, 2014.

Pratt, Laura. *Mountain Goats*. New York, N.Y.:
AV2 by Weigl, 2012.

Taylor, Sean. *Huck Runs Amuck!* New York, N.Y.:
Dial Books for Young Readers, 2011.

ON THE WEB
Learning more about mountain goats
is as easy as 1, 2, 3.

1. Go to www.factsurfer.com.

2. Enter "mountain goats" into the search box.

3. Click the "Surf" button and you will see a
   list of related web sites.

With factsurfer.com, finding more
information is just a click away.

Index

The images in this book are reproduced through the courtesy of: mlharing, front cover; Rocky Grimes, p. 4; Perspectives - Jeff Smith, p. 7; Steve Boice, p. 8; Rolf Nussbaumer Photography/ Alamy, pp. 9, 15; Matt Ragen, pp. 10-11; Prisma by Dukas Presseagentur GmbH/ Alamy, p. 12; Ekaterina Bykova, p. 13 (top left, bottom); Kenneth Rush, p. 13 (top center); Josh Schutz, p. 13 (top right); Walter Siegmund/ Wiki Commons, p. 14 (top left); Maxsol, p. 14 (top right); Olga Popova, p. 14 (center left); de2marco, p. 14 (center right); Noah Strycker, p. 14 (bottom left); emberiza, p. 14 (bottom right); Andrey Tarantin, p. 16; Sumio Harada/ Newscom, p. 17; robertharding/ Alamy, p. 18; DKVardiman, p. 19; Jon Eppard, p. 20; Donald M. Jones, p. 21.